DATE DUE			

NEW YORK

BRUCE GLASSMAN

THE
GREAT
CITIES
LIBRARY

A BLACKBIRCH PRESS BOOK

WOODBRIDGE, CONNECTICUT

Published by Blackbirch Press, Inc.
One Bradley Road, Suite 205
Woodbridge, CT 06525

Printed in Hong Kong
Bound in the United States of America

Editors: Kailyard Associates
Maps: Robert Italiano
Photo Research: Photosearch, Inc.

Library of Congress Cataloging-in-Publication Data

Glassman, Bruce.
  New York/Bruce Glassman.
  (The Great cities library)
  Includes bibliographical references and index.
  Summary: Describes the past, the people, and the things to see in the
various sections of Manhattan.
    ISBN 1-56711-024-X
    1. New York (N.Y.)—Geography—Juvenile literature. 2. New York (N.Y.)
—History—Juvenile literature. [1. Manhattan (New York, N.Y.)—Descrip-
tion.] I. Title.   II. Series: Great cities (New York, N.Y.)
F128.33.352 1990
917.47'1—dc20   90-1139
                                                          CIP
                                                          AC

pages 4–5
The East River skyline around midtown includes the U.N. Building, the Empire State Building, and the Chrysler Building.

CONTENTS

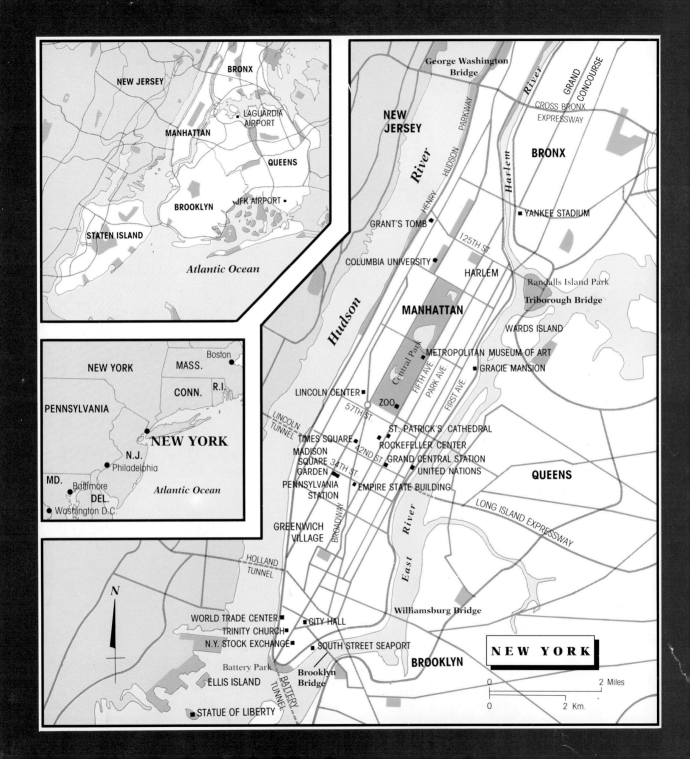

BRONX

NEW JERSEY

MANHATTAN

QUEENS

LAGUARDIA
AIRPORT

JFK AIRPORT

BROOKLYN

STATEN ISLAND

Atlantic Ocean

NEW YORK

MASS.
Boston

CONN.

R.I.

PENNSYLVANIA

NEW YORK

N.J.
Philadelphia

MD.
Baltimore

DEL.

Washington D.C.

Atlantic Ocean

George Washington
Bridge

**NEW
JERSEY**

GRAND
CONCOURSE

CROSS BRONX
EXPRESSWAY

BRONX

YANKEE STADIUM

Hudson River

Harlem River

HENRY HUDSON PARKWAY

GRANT'S TOMB

125TH ST.

COLUMBIA UNIVERSITY

HARLEM

Randalls Island Park

Triborough Bridge

MANHATTAN

Hudson River

Central Park

METROPOLITAN MUSEUM OF ART

GRACIE MANSION

WARDS ISLAND

FIFTH AVE.
PARK AVE.
FIRST AVE.

LINCOLN CENTER

ZOO

57TH ST.

ST. PATRICK'S CATHEDRAL

LINCOLN
TUNNEL

TIMES SQUARE

ROCKEFELLER CENTER

MADISON
SQUARE
GARDEN

42ND ST.

34TH ST.

GRAND CENTRAL STATION

UNITED NATIONS

QUEENS

PENNSYLVANIA
STATION

EMPIRE STATE BUILDING

LONG ISLAND EXPRESSWAY

**GREENWICH
VILLAGE**

BROADWAY

East River

HOLLAND
TUNNEL

N

Williamsburg Bridge

WORLD TRADE CENTER

CITY HALL

TRINITY CHURCH

N.Y. STOCK EXCHANGE

SOUTH STREET SEAPORT

Battery Park

**Brooklyn
Bridge**

BROOKLYN

BATTERY
TUNNEL

ELLIS ISLAND

STATUE OF LIBERTY

NEW YORK

0   2 Miles

0   2 Km.

Nickname: "The Big Apple"

Population: New York City: 7,086,096; Manhattan: 1,495,061.

Size: 300 square miles (New York City); 22.6 square miles (Manhattan)

Characteristics: The city has the largest population in the United States. Much of the land is surrounded by bays, rivers, and oceans. The island of Manhattan has one of the world's busiest harbors.

Average Temperature: 53° F. Average winter low: 25° F. Average snowfall: 27 inches per year. Average summer high: 83° F.

Government: The city is divided into five boroughs: Manhattan, Brooklyn, the Bronx, Queens, and Staten Island. Each borough has a president and within the boroughs there are district representatives. The borough presidents and the mayor make up the city council.

Location: The city's lands lie east of New Jersey, separated by the Hudson River. The southern ends of Brooklyn and Queens—as well as the eastern side of Staten Island—face the Atlantic Ocean. Northern Queens and the eastern and southern areas of the Bronx lie along the Long Island Sound.

Manhattan lies between the East River (east) and the Hudson River (west). The Harlem River runs to its north, with the Upper New York Bay to the south.

Ethnic Makeup: One of the most varied in the world. Contains large populations of almost every major ethnic group, including substantial numbers of Jews, African-Americans, Hispanics, Koreans, Indians, Italians, Irish, and Greeks. Other notable populations include Germans, Chinese, Caribbean peoples, Southeast Asians, Central Americans, and Eastern Europeans.

Main Industry: Brooklyn, Queens, and the Bronx thrive mostly on manufacturing and factory-related industries. Staten Island, though it contains some small businesses, is concerned mainly with the waste management industry. In Manhattan, the major industries are financial and cultural. Manhattan is one of the world's leading centers of finance and stock trading. It is also a world leader in various entertainment and mass communication industries such as television, book and magazine publishing, film, theater, dance, and opera.

THE PLACE

"The place was an island surrounded by oysters. Venison was so abundant that few troubled to breed sheep...The place was a gourmet's paradise and heavy eating became a New York tradition."

—V.S. Pritchett

Rockefeller Plaza offers an oasis of calm in the center of Manhattan.

8

JOHN·D·ROCKEFELLER·JR
1874-1960
FOUNDER OF ROCKEFELLER CENTER

The South Street Seaport, at the tip of Manhattan Island, preserves some of New York's maritime history.

New York City has long captured the imagination of people from all over the globe. It is one of the world's few cities—like Paris and London—that has a mystique all its own. The very image of New York, for most people, conjures up feelings of romance, glamour, and excitement—the thrill of a bustling metropolis where anything can happen.

In this book, when we speak of New York City, we are speaking mostly of the island of Manhattan. But New York City is technically made up of five boroughs: Brooklyn, Queens, the Bronx, Staten Island, and Manhattan. There is no dispute that—as far as fame and significance are concerned—Manhattan is the most important borough. Brooklyn can be found southeast of Manhattan, across the East River. Queens is located directly east of the island, also across the East River and connected to its south by Brooklyn. The Bronx is the borough to the north of Manhattan, and Staten Island is the borough due south.

New York Harbor is one of the largest and busiest in the world. It receives the water of seven rivers: the Hudson, Passaic, Hackensack, Raritan, Hutchinson, Bronx, and Newtown Creek.

There are many small islands surrounding the island of Manhattan. Liberty Island (which houses the famous statue), Ellis Island, and Governor's Island are all located at the harbor entrance. Others include Roosevelt Island, Randall's Island, Ward's

Island, and Riker's Island (where a city prison is located).

When you take the ferry from Staten Island to Manhattan, you see the city as it was first seen by the millions of immigrants who came to America. As you enter the New York Harbor you are greeted by America's most famous statue: The Statue of Liberty. Made of copper from a sculpture created by Italian artist Auguste Bartholdi, the green "Miss Liberty" weighs over 225 tons and stands more than 151 feet high.

Once you pass the Statue of Liberty and head for the pier, you may notice that Manhattan has its tallest buildings in only two areas of the island. One section is in the middle of the island and is known as "midtown." The other area is the southern end of the island, where Wall Street is located. These buildings are grouped together because they require foundations on bedrock, strong stone that goes deep into the earth. The southern end and the middle of Manhattan have the largest areas of bedrock.

Lower Manhattan: Wall Street, Lower East Side, Chinatown, and Little Italy

Wall Street is the heart of the financial industry—both for New York and for much of the world. It has many large, stone, Greek-influenced buildings as well as many modern skyscrapers. The New York Stock Exchange, which is on Wall Street, is a classic

The Statue of Liberty, one of the most famous landmarks in the world, stands on Liberty Island in New York harbor.

The Municipal Court Building

example of Greek Revival architecture, with its large stone columns and its triangle top. The most famous of the tall, modern buildings are the World Trade Towers, simple and sleek twin structures designed by Japanese architect Minoru Yamasaki. When they were first completed in 1974, these towers created an uproar from many New Yorkers who felt they ruined the famous skyline. Now, they're as much a part of Manhattan's unique skyline as the Empire State Building.

Even though many of the buildings in the southern end of Manhattan are quite modern, the narrow streets and winding alleys are reminiscent of old New York, when horse-drawn carriages bounced along on top of the city's cobble stone streets. This area also houses much of the city's and state's government buildings, most notably City Hall, Federal Hall, and the State Supreme Court building. Each of the buildings is a good example of Greek Revival architecture. City Hall has been called a "splendid little palace."

Between the Wall Street area and the Chelsea district (about a third of the island) are a number of ethnic neighborhoods. Many of the apartment houses and residences sit next to large warehouses and old factory buildings that used to house much of Manhattan's fabric and garment industry. In recent years, as space has become more and more precious on the island, restaurant and shop owners have taken advantage of these cavernous buildings by designing dramatic decors with high ceilings and large, open expanses.

The eastern section of this area is called the Lower East Side. It has traditionally been a Jewish enclave. Many Jewish immigrants at the turn of the century came here first before settling down elsewhere. There are very few new, modern buildings. The eighteenth-century brownstone and brick tenement houses still stand alongside synagogues, old-fashioned bakeries, and delicatessens.

To the west of the Lower East Side are two more distinctive areas. The more southern of the two is Chinatown; the northern is Little Italy. Like the Lower East Side, Chinatown seems stuck in the past. Cramped, dark produce markets and fish stores line the narrow streets. Vendors crowd the busy sidewalks. The smell of garlic and ginger wafts through the air and mingles with the blaring of horns and the constant babble of outdoor merchants eager to sell their wares.

Connected to Chinatown on the north is a small area known as Little Italy. Open-air *trattorias* (restaurants) line the streets, and small markets hang homemade sausages and parmesan, provolone, and mozzarella cheeses in their windows. There is a noticeable feeling of a family neighborhood in Little Italy. The classic brownstone apartment houses seem more lived-in, and there is less business activity

Shoppers in Chinatown

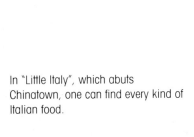

In "Little Italy", which abuts Chinatown, one can find every kind of Italian food.

on the streets. Within this area of a few blocks, one can find any kind of Italian food: the dense collection of restaurants and markets provide a bountiful supply of everything from carpaccio (very thin slices of raw beef or tuna) to cannoli (small cream-filled pastries).

Farther west, and stretching to the edge of the island, are the areas known as Greenwich Village and Soho. The term *soho* was created because the area is *SO*uth of *HO*uston (pronounced "how-stun") Street. These neighborhoods are popular for their many art galleries, antiques stores, funky restaurants, theaters, and clothing stores. In the sixties and seventies, many artists made their home in Soho's gigantic lofts and old factory buildings. "The Village," as it's known, takes its name from the small British town of Greenwich that was located here. Its reputation as a gathering place for writers and artists dates back to the nineteenth century, when such luminaries as Mark Twain and Henry James lived in the area.

Middle Manhattan: Chelsea and Midtown

Chelsea, the area around 23rd Street, begins to look quite different from the lower third of the island. The more human scale of downtown begins to give way to large office buildings. A few years ago, however, much of this area looked very similar to the warehouse districts of lower Manhattan. Rising real estate costs in midtown—and a general lack of space—forced many medium-sized businesses to seek less expensive space in this area. Today, Chelsea is a bustling neighborhood with movie theaters, modern restaurants, and fancy gourmet food shops.

Standing in the heart of Chelsea is the Flatiron Building—the world's first true skyscraper, and one of the city's most unique structures. Triangular in shape, the building stands on a concrete island—where Fifth Avenue crosses Broadway at 23rd Street. It remains one of the most distinctive New York landmarks.

The Flatiron Building has an unusual triangular design that fits the junction of Fifth Avenue and Broadway at 23rd Street.

WISDOM AND KNOWLEDGE SHALL BE THE STABILITY OF THY TIMES

The RCA Building at Rockefeller Center

To the east of the Flatiron is a small area called Gramercy Park. Large stone apartment houses and elegant brownstones recall the wealth of the area's past residents. Many of Manhattan's fanciest buildings surround Gramercy Park. The small park is enclosed by a black, wrought iron fence and is the heart of this area. Although a lovely respite from the concrete and steel of the city, the park is for residents only.

Not far from Chelsea and Gramercy Park, around 34th Street, the face of the city changes once again. Manhattan's streets become noticeably more congested and noisier. Tall buildings block the sun, making the area seem darker and colder. It is here that much of New York does its shopping. It is home to the famous department store Macy's, as well as many other major chains. Here, too, are Madison Square Garden and Penn Station, both busy locations where the flow of people seems never to let up.

Right off of Fifth Avenue on 34th Street stands one of New York's most famous and enduring symbols: the Empire State Building. When it was completed in 1931, it was the world's tallest building and remained so until 1974. But even without that distinction, it has no equal. Standing 102 stories (1,472 feet), it contains more than 60 miles of water pipes within its walls and supports 60,000 tons of structural steel. Twice a month, the 6,500 windows must be washed. Its design—a balance of graceful lines and Art Deco ornamentation—has made the Empire State Building an enduring symbol of New York's most glamorous and elegant age.

Further uptown, surrounded by large corporate and law offices, is the famous Chrysler Building. Completed in 1930 just before the Empire State Building, it was, for a short time, the world's tallest building. Hailed by many as the finest example of Art Deco architecture, the skyscraper is capped by a spire of six stainless steel arches housing triangular windows. It is particularly breathtaking when its spire, points, and triangles are lighted up at night.

Near the Chrysler Building is the entrance to the United Nations complex. It is here that diplomats from all over the world meet to discuss world problems and to negotiate peaceful settlements to conflicts between countries. On the outside, the complex is comprised of three seemingly unrelated buildings of very different modern styles.

Manhattan's midtown area continues north until about 59th Street, where Central Park begins. Between 42nd Street and 59th Street are some of the city's most expensive hotels, restaurants, and shops. This part of Manhattan is also the heart of the city's corporate business section. The Citicorp Building, located on east 53rd Street, is a fine example of sleek Post-Modernist architecture, with its bluish-gray steel exterior and slanted roof line. The AT&T Building, on east 55th Street, is an example of another

The statue of famed vaudeville star, George M. Cohan, stands in Times Square.

Central Park is an 843-acre green haven in the middle of the city.

trend in Post-Modernist design, one that blends earlier styles with modern styles. This pinkish marble building is topped with a Chippendale cornice, a distinctive design element that was popular with furniture makers of the 1700s.

A few blocks north of the AT&T building, "the grand-daddy of all American landscaped parks" begins. Central Park, an 843-acre tract of undeveloped land, sits smack in the middle of the island. To Frederick Law Olmsted, co-designer of the park, it was to be a place where young and old, rich and poor, could find a place to relax from the hectic pace of city life. When work was started in 1858, Central Park encompassed some of the swampiest, rockiest terrain in Manhattan. Given that, the design and beauty of the park is all the more stunning, with its hills, meadows, gardens, and woods. The area is filled with lakes and ponds, bridges, a boathouse, fountains, zoos, an ice skating rink, a carousel, sculptures, softball fields, bicycle paths, a theater, and a band shell. And there are countless pockets of isolated greenery that offer the visitor a chance to escape the steel and concrete jungle.

In the summer, when temperatures average in the 80s and 90s, New Yorkers crowd the Sheep Meadow to suntan and play frisbee on the grass. During the winter, when temperatures average in the teens, both youngsters and adults enjoy the Wollman Ice Skating Rink and sledding down the park's steep hills. A horse-and-carriage ride through the park in the fall, when the leaves are changing and the air is cool and crisp, is one of the most popular activities the park has to offer.

The Upper East Side and the Upper West Side

The face of the city changes once again as midtown turns into residential neighborhoods on either side of the park. The city to the east of Central Park is known as the East Side and is comprised of stately old brownstones and townhouses that today are affordable only to the very wealthy. Korean produce markets and open-air bistros are common sights on the East Side, along with specialty food and clothing shops. The tree-lined neighborhood streets are often

The Central Park Zoo is a popular tourist attraction.

The Metropolitan Museum, on Fifth Avenue, houses one of the country's most important art collections.

clean and quiet refuges from the dirt and noise of midtown Manhattan.

On the other side of the park—the West Side—the neighborhoods have a different flavor than those of the East Side. This is home to many of the city's middle-class and upwardly mobile young people. Many writers and artists are attracted to the West Side because of its multi-ethnic character and somewhat more modest rentals than the East Side. Columbus Avenue, which runs down near the west side of Central Park, is known for its whimsical and exotic shops that sell arts and crafts, modern furniture, and "hip"—but expensive—clothing.

Much of the rest of the island on both sides of Central Park and in northern Manhattan is residential. A number of notable buildings, such as the modern Guggenheim Museum, the Museum of Natural History, the Cooper Hewitt Museum, and the Whitney Museum are located in the northern section of the Upper East Side. The scenic community on Riverside Drive in the northern section of the West Side by the Hudson River is filled with imposing stone buildings that feature high windows and lots of wrought iron.

Above Central Park: Morningside Heights, Harlem, Washington Heights

Just above Central Park on the Upper West Side is where Columbia University begins. Tucked into the city streets, the university is a highly respected institution that offers an impressive range of programs, many of which involve using the great resources of the city that surrounds it.

Northern Manhattan—from about 125th Street to 207th Street—is a great mix of neighborhoods and cultures. Many think of this part of the island as a "no man's land," a dangerous and mysterious place, and for those who are not familiar with its workings it can be rather overwhelming. For many years, the Harlem area has been one of the country's saddest examples of urban decay, poverty, and crime. The area's story is particularly sad given its glorious past. In the 1920s, 1930s, and 1940s, Harlem was a glittering community filled with fancy nightclubs, restaurants, and businesses. Jazz and blues music, in particular, flourished in Harlem, and a large number of the world's great jazz musicians have come out of the Harlem tradition. Beautiful brownstone buildings lined the wide streets of this buzzing, electric neighborhood in the early decades of the twentieth century.

Though the area still has its troubles, there are signs of change. Neighborhoods are being rebuilt. Many of Harlem's most elegant buildings are being restored to their previous grandeur. And a number of well-respected dance and theater companies have surfaced (most notably the Alvin Ailey dance company and the Dance Troupe of Harlem), partly in an effort to bring the arts back to the area. Harlem's mix of cultures, which includes African, Caribbean, Cuban, Puerto Rican, and Colombian, offers the curious visitor an impressive potential to experience the food, history, and culture of these ethnic heritages. A number of museums in Harlem (described in more detail in the "On the Tour Bus" section) have interesting exhibits and programs on black and Hispanic cultures as well.

How Manhattan is Organized

In the southern section of the island—the Wall Street and Chinatown area—there is no easy way to understand the layout of the streets. Each street is named rather than numbered, and many don't run all the way east or west, north or south. Some run along a diagonal, others stop and start up again a few blocks later. The best strategy for lower Manhattan is to always have a map handy!

Above 8th Street or so, things become a good deal easier. Here, the simple grid system begins. Running across the island (east to west), the streets are numbered. As you head north (uptown), the street numbers get higher. Running the length of the island (north and south) are the avenues. Some of the avenues are numbered, others are named. Fifth Avenue is used as the dividing line between the east side and the west side of the island. The number in a given address will get higher as it moves farther away from Fifth Avenue. For example, "10 West 42nd Street" will be right off Fifth Avenue on the west side of Fifth Avenue. An address such as "340 West 42nd Street" will be three or four avenues west of Fifth Avenue. The grid system is how most of the island north of 8th street is organized.

How People Get Around

There are many means of transportation in New York City. With all the congestion during the daylight hours, walking is often the most efficient means available. Buses and subways cover most of the island and can be the fastest way of traveling longer distances. The buses are mostly clean and modern, though they fall prey to the oppressive traffic that plagues the city. The New York subway is the largest city electrical railway system in the world. It connects all of New York's boroughs, except Staten Island, and covers more than 220 miles. Though much of the system is badly in need of repair and modernization, a good deal of work has been done in the past few years to improve service and upgrade trains. Taxis are a luxury, both because they are quite expensive and because they are often hard to get.

The Other Boroughs

Though Manhattan has the greatest concentration of sights and attractions, there are many notable

The New York City subway system is one of the world's largest, with over 200 miles of track.

things to be seen in Brooklyn, Queens, the Bronx, and Staten Island. Given the "stardom" of Manhattan Island the high points of the other boroughs are often ignored.

Brooklyn

The area just over the Brooklyn Bridge, which is northern Brooklyn, is one of the city's most beautiful and popular neighborhoods. Known as Brooklyn Heights, and once nicknamed "Borough of Churches," this tree-lined area has an extensive historic district, which includes some fine, nineteenth-century churches. Victorian townhouses are nestled along the East River, just across the water

Manhattan Island is connected to Brooklyn by a series of bridges.

from Lower Manhattan. The Promenade winds along the bay and river, offering an ideal spot for viewing the Manhattan skyline.

Brooklyn is the most heavily populated borough and contains a wide variety of neighborhoods. Like any other major metropolitan area, they range from slums to suburbs, with everything in between. Prospect Park, located in northern mid-Brooklyn, is a favorite of local residents. It features a large natural expanse of greenery and lakes with an abundance of recreational activities.

Brooklyn's most famous site is undoubtedly Coney Island. An island in name only, it has drawn crowds of people for almost a hundred years to its beach and amusement park. The Coney Island hot dog came to typify the essentially American spirit found here in Brooklyn. It is this spirit that has made Brooklyn such a popular setting over the years for movies, plays, novels, and TV shows.

The Brooklyn Bridge was one of the engineering marvels of the nineteenth century.

Queens

The largest of the five boroughs, Queens was once a quiet collection of different towns and developments begun after the Civil War. Even with the annexation of Queens to New York in 1898 and the rapid development that followed within a decade, there is a remarkably different feel to each community. Though the borough lacks the large open spaces characteristic of the Bronx, the residential areas are

Astoria, in Queens, is home to a large Greek-American population.

threaded with gardens and "greenbelts." To the borough's good fortune, architects and developers alike strove for a different kind of city than the one that sprouted up across the East River.

Most of Queens is made up of medium to small factories and middle-income residential neighborhoods. Long Island City, along the East River directly across from Manhattan's midtown area, has until recently been blocks of warehouses, outlets, and manufacturing facilities. Today, the area is fast becoming a haven for artists and other people who desire large living spaces and can't pay Manhattan prices.

Like the Lower East Side almost a century before, immigrants have streamed to the neighborhoods of Queens, only here the mix is more diverse and the economic situation more prosperous. There is almost no match for the variety of food offerings, and without the high prices of Manhattan.

The Bronx

The Bronx, while larger than either Manhattan or Staten Island, is about half the size of Brooklyn and only about a third the size of Queens. Situated at the northern boundary of the city, it is the only borough on the mainland. The Bronx, in many ways, was the first and nearest suburb to Manhattan. It has always been an interesting mix of wealthy and working-class neighborhoods.

The Bronx is perhaps best known for its baseball team (the Yankees) and outstanding zoo (the nation's largest urban zoo). But within the gently rolling hills of the borough are to be found a 250-acre botanical garden and many large and beautiful parks, as well as stately mansions and grand estates.

Staten Island

The borough of Staten Island is located southwest of Manhattan, across the Upper New York Bay. The island appears very different from any of its fellow boroughs, for there are few areas of concentrated population and no "city" to be seen.

Many of the island's residential areas are located along the rim of the island. These tree-lined neighborhoods are filled with houses that often sit on small front lawns and overlook a harbor or a pier. Small Italian grocery stores serve local residents who are known for their close-knit communities and neighborhood pride.

A great deal of Staten Island has been set aside by the city government to perform the task of managing the city's waste. Garbage barges from Manhattan regularly tow the island's massive amounts of trash to dumps and landfills on Staten Island. Though never popular with residents of Staten Island, it is an unavoidable and essential need that must be fulfilled in order to keep Manhattan, and the rest of New York City, alive.

THE PAST

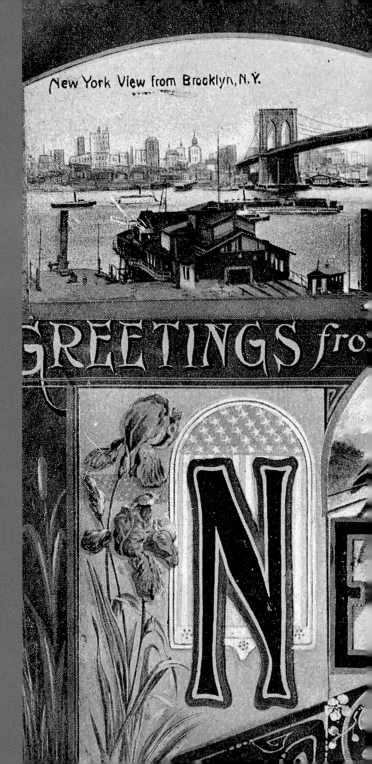

*"If I can make it there, I'll make it any-
where."*
        —From the song "New York, New York"

A 1908 postcard extolls the pleasures of a trip to New
York City.

View of New-York Bay.

Misty Morning on New York Bay.

N-YORK

Statue of Liberty
N.Y. City.

talian navigator Giovanni da Verrazano first discovered New York Bay in 1524, as he searched for a northwest passage around the world. Eighty-five years later, in 1609, an English explorer named Henry Hudson—who was sailing for the Dutch— took his ship the *Half Moon* more than 100 miles northward, up the river that now bears his name.

By the 1620s, Dutch colonists had settled on the lower part of Manhattan Island. In 1625, a permanent settlement was established on the southern tip of the island, called New Netherland, with the central town of New Amsterdam as its capital. It was colonized primarily as a trading post for the Dutch West India Company. A year later, Dutch leader Peter Minuit bought the island from the Manhattan Indians, part of the Algonquin Nation. Minuit bargained for the island with trinkets and finally secured possession with merchandise worth approximately $24.

For the nearly 40 years that followed, the new colony prospered and its population grew steadily. In 1639, Jonas Bronck settled the wild area north of the Harlem River, the land now known as the Bronx. During the next decade, settlements were established in Brooklyn, Queens (the first in Flushing in 1643), and Staten Island.

By 1653, members of the Dutch West India Company incorporated the island as a city—officially known as New Amsterdam. A year later, in 1654,

New Amsterdam was the home of the first permanent Jewish settlement in North America. A protec-
tive wall was erected around the inner limits of the
city to guard against invasion and sudden attack.
This is the area that we now know as Wall Street.

The harsh and unpredictable weather on the island
was a hardship for the earliest settlers. Heavy snows
and freezing temperatures made their small wooden
houses uncomfortable during the long winters. Yet,
the excellent bay and harbor that served the island
enabled it to prosper like no other.

As the colonies grew, they became more prosperous. This prosperity, however, also invited conflict.
The English noticed the new wealth of the Dutch and
decided they needed to acquire it. In 1664, the Duke
of York sent a British fleet into New York harbor to
take possession of New Amsterdam. Unable to
organize a successful defense, the city surrendered to
the English, who renamed it New York. Conflicts
continued between the British and the Dutch for
more than a decade before the island was officially
ceded to England by treaty. Even after the island
was given over, minor battles continued to be waged
against British rule. In 1689, Jacob Leisler led an
insurrection against the British governors, which
ended in defeat for the Dutch.

After the city received its first charter from James
II in 1686, the first City Hall, later called Federal
Hall, was built at Broad and Wall streets. The New

Looking down Wall Street toward
Brooklyn Heights, 1834

York *Gazette* was the city's first official newspaper, founded in 1725. John Peter Zenger followed nine years later with an opposition newspaper, the *Weekly Journal*. But Zenger was soon charged with acts of sedition for publishing articles very critical of the British administration. He was tried and acquitted in a trial that set the legal precedent for freedom of the press.

The following years saw a large increase in slave population on the island. This was primarily due to the fact that much of the business that was done by the Dutch and the British stemmed from trade connections with Africa. By 1754, the population of New York had grown to more than 16,000 people.

In 1765, the Stamp Act Congress met in New York, making the city an official center of colonial opposition to British domination. Soon, conflicts over British rule began to arise in the colonies all along the Northeast. The Boston Massacre of 1770 further heightened tensions that fueled the American Revolution, which began in 1775.

The Revolutionary War Era

The island of Manhattan served as a colonial headquarters for General George Washington during the American Revolution. Though much of the most decisive fighting took place in nearby New Jersey, a few important revolutionary war battles were fought in the New York area. The most notable of these battles was the Battle of Long Island, in which the British captured more than a thousand men and killed or wounded hundreds more. Though this battle did little to enhance General Washington's reputation as a commander, he did manage to save his army from being completely destroyed. The British, headquartered on Staten Island, won most of the skirmishes fought on New York City soil and managed to occupy the area for the last few years of the war. By 1778, the Revolution had taken its toll on the island. Two mysterious fires, one in 1776 and the other two years later, virtually destroyed the entire city.

After the war was over, the colonists set their minds to organizing a new government. By 1789, the United States had elected its first president—General George Washington—who was sworn in at Federal Hall in Manhattan. The island, which was the first state capital until 1796, also served as the first capital of the federal government from 1789 to 1790.

The first U.S. census in 1790 recorded more than 33,000 people in New York City. Growth, peace, and prosperity continued until 1812, when war against Britain erupted again, and New York City was blockaded. The War of 1812 started as a result of conflicts over American-Canadian boundaries and maritime rights to the Great Lakes and the Mississippi. It ended in 1814 with the signing of the Treaty of Ghent.

Lower Broadway and St. Paul's Chapel around 1798.

A view of New York's busy
harbor, 1878

By 1825, the Erie Canal gave another boost to New York's already busy seaports. Commercial vessels could now travel north up the Hudson River all the way to Lake Erie. This new waterway not only connected the Atlantic Ocean to the Great Lakes, it caused a terrific boon in industry all along the Hudson River and made New York's ports and harbor more valuable than ever.

Between 1830 and 1860, New York City grew at an astounding rate. By 1834, the city of Brooklyn was incorporated and, by 1840, New York had become the busiest and most important seaport in the nation. In 1858, work on Central Park was begun, though it would take nearly 20 years to complete.

The Great Wave of Immigration

A massive wave of German and Irish immigrants flooded New York from 1830 to 1860. Often poverty-stricken and in poor health, many of these immigrants brought with them diseases from other countries. Epidemics of yellow fever and cholera devastated the city during this period and were only worsened by the island's poor water supply and often unsanitary living conditions.

This great wave of immigration swelled the city's population to 750,000 by the eve of the Civil War in 1861. On the whole, New York City was barely affected by the war over slavery being fought to the south. Though New York took the side of the Union and sent many of its residents to fight—as did most northeastern states—the fighting did not come as far as New York City. In 1863, however, riots protesting the Federal Conscription Act of the Civil War broke out in the streets of the city. This caused widespread unrest throughout New York.

Soon after the Civil War, New York experienced another surge of immigration. This time, the newcomers were mostly Italians and Eastern Europeans. A great many of these immigrants found work on the city's numerous large construction projects, such as the Brooklyn Bridge (started in 1869 and completed in 1883), the elevated railroad on Third Avenue (completed in 1868, but no longer there), and the Statue of Liberty (started in France in 1865 and

Ellis Island was the first stop for millions of immigrants. It has now been restored and is a national monument.

unveiled 20 years later in 1885). By the turn of the century, the island was home to a crowded but varied mass of citizens, and the population was still growing rapidly.

The City of New York was established and incorporated into five boroughs in 1898: Manhattan, Brooklyn, Queens, Bronx, and Staten Island. The area encompassed over 300 square miles and was home to over three million people. In order to more effectively move its residents from place to place, New York's first underground electric railway was opened

Mulberry Street, the heart of "Little Italy," on New York's Lower East Side, 1906

in 1904. This subway system was soon expanded to its present-day size.

Immigrants continued to pour in from all over the world in search of a better life in the United States. The city's population exploded. The island's resources became strained and living conditions in the most heavily populated areas—such as the Lower East Side and the West Side between 30th and 50th Streets (known as Hell's Kitchen)—worsened considerably. These neighborhoods, which were lined with poorly built tenement houses, were greatly overburdened by newly arrived immigrants. In some cases, 10 or 20 people packed themselves into an apartment. Sewage and sanitation facilities could not meet the demand placed upon them by the overcrowding. Often, the summertime heat and stagnant air would create a stench powerful enough to make many a passerby faint. And the streets became increasingly more dangerous as out-of-work or poorly paid citizens became more desperate to survive in a city that was quickly reaching the limit of its resources. Movements advocating restrictions on immigration began to take hold but did little to stem the flood of people that arrived each day.

In 1914, World War I disrupted the forward progress of cities all across the country. As the nation dedicated itself to production for the war effort, many everyday items that had been plentiful in the great harbor city became scarce. Still, New

York—with its newspapers and influential personalities—proved invaluable to helping the war effort as a center of morale-boosting for the entire country.

At the end of the war in 1918, New York switched gears and devoted itself to the modernization efforts that had been interrupted by the war. The following decade proved to be a time of great change. Various political movements swept across the nation. One of these was Prohibition, which was the passage of a law banning the consumption of alcohol. Another was Women's Suffrage, which advocated women's right to vote. This was also a period of great optimism in the country.

In Harlem, a great burst of creative activity began to take hold. Black writers were finally being recognized by publishers and a nonblack audience. Though Harlem was at the center of a thriving black literary community, it also attracted painters, sculptors, and musicians. Harlem nightclubs and dance halls were full of an energetic new sound—jazz—and the entire area flourished as a center of style, artistic creativity, and great business opportunity. On almost any summer night one could hear the cool sounds of jazz masters like Duke Ellington, Count Basie, or Ella Fitzgerald wafting down the streets as tall, slender women wrapped in furs and jewels were escorted down the avenue by wide-shouldered, swanky men in "zoot suits" (stylish men's suits of the period).

Herald Square at Broadway and 34th Street, 1909

The great war was now over, and many Americans were back home with their families. A feeling of contentment and security seemed to roll across the nation. Americans were investing in businesses and the stock market in great numbers—each sure that their American Dream would come true and they would turn into millionaires overnight. Some of those dreamers were right, but, on October 29, 1929, many people's dreams turned into nightmares. It was on that day the stock market crashed on Wall Street, throwing the country—and then much of the world—into the Great Depression.

The Depression lasted for about 10 years and devastated much of the country. Breadlines 10 blocks long became common city sights. And tarpaper shacks and cardboard lean-tos cropped up in many public spaces, as more and more Americans were forced to give up their homes. While the Depression was seriously felt in the city, New York still managed to move forward—though a good deal more slowly—during this period. The city had been such a heavy center of business and industry before the Crash that much of the business that did survive the Depression survived in and around New York.

New York politics, from the 1860s until the early 1930s, was plagued by corrupt city government. At the heart of the problem was the iron-handed dominance of the Tammany Hall group—a large flock of "insider" politicians who sold favors and

The New York Stock Exchange is downtown in the most historic area of Manhattan Island.

peddled their influence throughout the city. The Democratic machine, headed by William Marcy "Boss" Tweed, ruthlessly exploited his control of the local government, small businesses, and many other aspects of the city. Tweed and his cronies were convicted of misappropriation of funds in 1871 largely through the efforts of Samuel Tilden, later governor of New York, and the acid cartoons of Thomas Nast. The corrupt political ring, however, was not finally dismantled until Samuel Seabury headed an investigation that exposed the practices of Tammany and forced mayor Jimmy Walker to resign, in 1932.

Finally rid of the tyranny of Tammany Hall, the citizens of the city elected a spunky politician named Fiorello LaGuardia as their mayor in 1933.

LaGuardia vowed to clean up New York City government and to work hard to create effective social reforms. An energetic and inspirational leader, LaGuardia became one of the most popular mayors in the city's history. All in all, he served three terms and remained in office for 11 years, until 1945.

It was during the Depression era of the 1930s, when the Art Deco movement was at its greatest popularity, that the Empire State Building, the Chrysler Building, and Radio City Music Hall were completed. New York also became a major center for the moviemaking industry, one business that remained popular despite the country's troubling times.

The Palestine Exhibition Hall at The
New York World's Fair, 1939

The end of the Depression and U.S. involvement in
World War II coincided. However, before the nation
became totally enmeshed in the war, it enjoyed
hearing about and seeing the 1939 World's Fair at
Flushing Meadows in Queens. The Fair introduced
to a curious and economically battered nation new
technologies that provided an exciting glimpse of the
future.

By 1941, with the Japanese attack on Pearl Harbor,
the United States was fully involved in World War II,
and New York City, as it did during World War I,
geared up for war production and wartime rationing
of food and other goods. Aside from the frequent
blackouts and shortages, neither New York City
nor the rest of the country were greatly affected by
the war. The 1940s remained a time of increasing
prosperity for Americans, and after the end of the

war in 1945, a period of rapid growth that has few parallels in this nation's history began.

In 1952, New York City raised its status as one of the world's most international and important cities. It was in that year that the United Nations headquarters opened its doors on the city's East Side. John D. Rockefeller, Jr., had donated the site along the East River where the three main buildings of the complex were built. Since that time, the United Nations headquarters has served as a meeting place for diplomats and envoys from countries all over the world. In those buildings, international leaders strive to resolve conflicts and disputes through negotiation and compromise rather than aggression and war.

Unfortunately, the U.N. has not been able to stop all conflict. U.S. forces became embroiled in a military conflict in Korea that had begun in 1950. The Korean War was fought over the dividing line between North and South Korea. Involving many American troops as well as smaller forces from 13 other nations, the war was not resolved until 1953.

The Korean conflict helped to provoke a period in America—between 1950 and 1954—when fear of communism reached hysterical proportions. This period is now known as the "McCarthy Era." In 1950, Wisconsin Senator Joseph McCarthy announced that there were 205 Communists in the State Department. His claim created a wave of paranoia that swept across the nation and dragged

In the 1940s, The Brooklyn Dodgers and The New York Yankees were fierce baseball rivals.

with it many innocent people who were falsely accused of espionage or subversion against America. New York City, given its large population of artists, writers, and "free thinkers," was among the cities most affected by the "Red Scare." The "Blacklist," which was a published listing of all Americans who were suspected of being Communists, ruined many acting and writing careers—and affected many of New York's most prominent artists.

Modern New York

For the most part, the rest of the 1950s was quiet, both for New York City and for the rest of the country. Americans were fed up with the destruction and disruption of war and were hoping for a chance to enjoy peace and prosperity for a while. By the 1960s, however, new problems threatened the calm surface of American life.

The United States was getting deeply involved in a war in a small Asian country called Vietnam. New York and other major cities became centers of protest and demonstration against the war. Central Park frequently served as a large meeting area for antiwar protestors, and many of New York's residents used their city's high visibility to spread their messages of peace and noninvolvement. Vietnam was not the only issue on people's minds during the 1960s. New York, as well as San Francisco, Chicago, and Washington, often served as a key meeting place

The United Nations Building was opened in 1952 on a site donated by John D. Rockefeller, Jr.

The twin towers of The World Trade Center dominate the skyline of Lower Manhattan.

for political gatherings. Large demonstrations for civil rights and women's rights were frequent sights the city in the sixties.

At the helm of the city's government during this turbulent time was the charismatic and charming John V. Lindsay. Elected in 1965, he was the first Republican to hold the office in over 20 years. Responding to New York's growing economic problems, he was the first New York mayor to institute a city income tax. Though the city experienced some long-ranging financial hardships during his tenure, Lindsay was notable for his ability to keep New York City relatively calm during the late 1960s. While other major cities across the country were experiencing destructive race riots, New York City remained functional and, for the most part, peaceful. Though some rioting did occur, particularly in Harlem, the city remained intact, unlike Chicago, Los Angeles, and Atlanta.

By 1970, a wave of real estate development was washing over Manhattan. Some of this was due to the modernization and building in Battery Park, at the southern tip of the island, where the World Trade Center Complex was being erected. By 1974, the twin towers had been completed and lower Manhattan would never look the same.

Manhattan's land prices rose quickly. A steady stream of new residents caused the housing market to swell, and living space became scarce. The city contained more people than it did decent apartments. As the price of housing rose above the means of many people, ghettos and run-down neighborhoods became more noticeable throughout the city. At the same time, the city experienced serious budget problems. With a shrinking tax base and the cost of public services beginning to rise dramatically, New York City faced possible bankruptcy. As an emergency measure, the city established the Municipal Assistance Corporation, which turned around and lent the city the funds it needed to survive. Then, under the leadership of Mayor Edward I. Koch, taxes were raised, thousands of city government jobs were eliminated, and city services were significantly reduced in order to reestablish the city's credit.

Although New York was not the only city facing bankruptcy, its problems seemed larger. Things got worse in the 1980s. Under Mayor Koch, Manhattan real estate continued to be sold to large companies for renovation and eventual re-sale in very expensive markets. Co-op apartments and condominiums sprouted up all over the city, forcing many middle- and low-income residents to move out of the city or into less desirable—often dangerous and run-down— neighborhoods.

Koch, an outspoken and colorful politician, defended New York's development as a means of supporting its ever-growing financial problems. But as a result of the skyrocketing prices of real estate, the

Federal Hall, site of Washington's inauguration as the first president of the United States

city soon became a place where only the super-rich or the poor could live. By the middle to the end of the eighties, real estate had become so expensive that many large businesses were leaving the city for Connecticut or New Jersey, where corporate office space and operating costs would be drastically cheaper. With those businesses went important tax revenues.

Despite many of the city's problems during Koch's tenure, he was a popular mayor. Elected a total of three times, he served from 1977-1989. In many ways, the troubles of the city were not all his doing; he had inherited a great number of them from previous mayors. Koch's final years in office, however, were rocked by many serious scandals. The most notorious were instances of corruption on the part of some of the mayor's closest associates. Other scandals, such as the discovery of "insider trading" on Wall Street—most notably by Ivan Boesky—did little to boost New York's image as a fair and friendly place.

The mayoral election of 1989 heralded a change in the city's government. That year David N. Dinkins, New York's first black mayor, was elected. Calm and composed, Dinkins offers a very different style for running city hall.

Although Dinkins's election gave minorities in the city new hope and power, having a black mayor did little to calm the city's growing racial tensions. In

fact, racial attacks, prejudice, and divisiveness between ethnic groups continue to be serious problems
in the city.

As is common in any large city, drugs, crime, and
homelessness plague New York, as they have for
years. Serious problems of air and water pollu-
tion—as well as widespread graffiti, littering, and
vandalism of public property— remain growing
threats to the health and well-being of each and
every New Yorker.

Many solutions have been offered through the
decades, but few have ever come to pass. Yet, the
majority of the city's residents remain confident that
the city can survive. Its enormous base of culture,
ethnic groups, tourist attractions, and business
promise to sustain much of New York's prosperity.
As the financial capital for much of the United
States, Manhattan will also remain vital for its in-
vestment markets as well as its business in insur-
ance, real estate, and communications.

Under the leadership of David Dinkins, the city
faces many tough choices for the future. The costs
of running New York City have risen steadily over
the years and have far outpaced tax increases. Fund-
ing for schools, city services, and welfare programs
are continuing to dry up. And, though new ideas
about how to spend city money are starting to come
forth, the real impact of the city's new mayor is yet
to be felt.

David Dinkins was elected the first
African-American mayor of New York,
in 1989.

THE PEOPLE

"Although New Yorkers of all kinds curse the city for its expense and its pressures, and though all foreigners think it is the other foreigners who make it impossible, they are mad about the place. There is no other place like it in the world."

—V.S. Pritchett

The energy and ethnic diversity of New York City's population has long been one of its most important resources.

A street musician on Fifth Avenue

Since the time of the Dutch settlers, Manhattan has been well known for welcoming newcomers of all nationalities. As one of the world's best and busiest ports, New York has historically experienced a constant flow of people from all over the world. Immigrants from years past knew there was a place for them in the city that was truly America's most concentrated melting pot. For them, New York meant the hope of opportunity in a community filled with people from the same background, struggling with the same problems.

During the early 1800s, a great majority of Irish, German, and Norwegian immigrants sailed to New York's shores. Toward the end of that century, Russian Jews and Poles began to arrive in great numbers. By the turn of the century, large numbers of blacks from the South sought better job opportunities and more hospitable social conditions.

Today, the city continues to be home to a kaleidoscope of cultures. Chinese and Korean populations have grown rapidly in the past 50 years. And island cultures from the Caribbean and the Bahamas have grown steadily in recent times.

Manhattan's population today is roughly 53 percent white, 21 percent Hispanic, 20 percent black, and 5 percent Asian/Pacific Islander. About 1 percent of the city's population is American Indian. The largest three single-ancestry groups are English (4 percent), Irish (4 percent), and Italian (4 percent).

For the more established ethnic groups, Manhattan has traditionally offered specific areas where each culture predominates. This, of course, was not by law but rather because newcomers often prefer to set up their new homes among people of their own culture.

Chinatown, in lower Manhattan, is a clearly defined area where the Chinese language and culture remains well preserved. Here, almost any kind of traditional Chinese food can be bought in open-air markets or by vendors along Canal Street. Butcher shops that specialize in duck, chicken, and spare ribs can be found on almost every street, along with fish markets and produce stands that carry everything from bok choy (Chinese leafy green vegetable), to sesame oil.

Directly above Chinatown, in Little Italy, shopkeepers, waiters, and residents can be heard speaking their native Italian in the typically clean and cozy markets and restaurants. Small corner shops display large, freshly made cheeses in their windows, along with cured and smoked meats and freshly baked breads. As in Italy, each street houses a shop that specializes in one area of food, and residents must travel from shop to shop to get the freshest and most delicious items from each expert producer.

Further to the east, the streets are filled with New Yorkers of Eastern European descent, mostly Jews, who have traditionally made their homes on

A young Chinese-American New Yorker

A food market in the vicinity of Union Square

Manhattan's Lower East Side. Here, delicatessens serve up steaming pastrami or corned beef on rye and bakeries beckon with the unmistakable smell of hot, fresh bagels.

A bit farther north, around 6th Street on the East Side, an enclave of Indian restaurants can be found. This area is known to many New Yorkers as "Little India" and offers authentic Indian cuisine (often accompanied by live music) as well as spice shops that carry items from India.

There are many other areas throughout the city that offer ethnic food. Thai restaurants are popular and can be found in the midtown area on the West Side. A variety of Afghani and Turkish restaurants can also be found in the same area.

The great variety of cultures in New York City has led to its longstanding reputation as one of the world's best places for fine dining. Many of the finest chefs from France, Italy, China, and other countries around the globe have traditionally come to New York to work. It offers them high pay as well as a sophisticated and eager clientele to serve. Inch for inch, New York probably offers more top class restaurants than any other city in the world.

Famous New York Figures

Manhattan and its surrounding boroughs have been the birthplace of countless famous people throughout history. Theodore "Teddy" Roosevelt was born on 20th Street in 1858 and spent the first 15 years of his life growing up in the Gramercy Park neighborhood. Peter Cooper, one of the country's most famous inventor-manufacturer-philanthropists, was born in Manhattan in 1791. Shirley Chisholm, the first black woman elected to the U.S. House of Representatives, was born in Brooklyn in 1924.

Pulitzer Prize-winning playwright Eugene O'Neill, born in New York City, is credited by many with raising the American theater (particularly Broadway) "to adulthood." O'Neill's bleak, emotionally dark dramas (such as *Long Day's Journey into Night* and *The Iceman Cometh*) changed the nature of theater in the United States in the early 1900s from a simple diversion to a powerful and moving art form.

Eugene O'Neill, 1937

Lena Horne, 1985, accepting her Eubie Award

Harlem-born dramatist Arthur Miller also did much to change the face of American theater. During his most prolific period, just after World War II, Miller, like Eugene O'Neill, produced penetrating psychological dramas that challenged the general public's taste for simple, happy musicals. Miller, who has spent most of his life in the New York City area, is most famous for his Pulitzer Prize-winning play *Death of a Salesman*, which was the first contemporary drama to present a "common man" as a tragic hero.

Poet and philanthropist Emma Lazarus, born in New York City, wrote many works in defense of Judaism and became an advocate for the rights and freedoms of immigrants during the late 1800s. She is most famous for her sonnet "The New Colossus," which is inscribed on a tablet at the base of the Statue of Liberty. Other writers, such as James Baldwin (*The Fire Next Time*), Herman Melville (*Moby Dick*), Edith Wharton (*Ethan Frome*), and Washington Irving (*Legend of Sleepy Hollow*) were all born in New York City.

Many famous actors and celebrities were also born in the Big Apple. Among them are Danny Aiello, Alan Alda, Bea Arthur, Lauren Bacall, Harry Belafonte, Pat Benetar, Mel Brooks, George Burns, Phoebe Cates, Chevy Chase, Tony Danza, Sammy Davis, Jr., Robert DeNiro, Neil Diamond, Jane Fonda, Mel Gibson, Rita Hayworth, Gregory Hines,

Lena Horne, Billy Joel, Cyndi Lauper, Eddie Murphy, Al Pacino, Rob Reiner, Jerome Robbins, Brooke Shields, Beverly Sills, Carly Simon, Sylvester Stallone, Cicely Tyson, and Billy Dee Williams.

More important than who was born in New York City, however, are the many people who have become an important part of the city's identity. Many renowned writers and editors, such as Horace Greeley, Dorothy Parker, Edna St. Vincent Millay, and Henry Miller, often used New York as the subject or the setting for some of their finest work. Present-day writers such as Tom Wolfe (*Bonfire of the Vanities),* Jay McInerny (*Bright Lights, Big City),* and Tama Janowitz (*Slaves of New York)* have become popular for their contemporary portrayals about life in Manhattan.

New York-based actor and singer Paul Robeson enriched Broadway and the New York music scene for many years with his stunning baritone voice and his commanding stage presence, most notable in his role as the emperor in Eugene O'Neill's *The Emperor Jones* and in the title role of Shakespeare's *Othello.* Brooklyn-born actor-writer-director Woody Allen has also focused much of his career on and in New York. His many movies, stand-up comedy routines, and novels have both made fun of and romanticized New York lifestyles and New York people.

New York natives George and Ira Gershwin, with their uplifting and popular musicals, did much in the

Pop-vocalist, Cyndi Lauper

Art Garfunkel *(left)* and Paul Simon *(right)* created some of the most memorable music of the sixties.

1920s and 1930s to keep the romantic vision of Manhattan alive. The jazz craze that swept through Harlem in the twenties and thirties (and then through the rest of the world) was fueled by such great New York musical talents as Duke Ellington, Pearl Baily, Count Basie, Ella Fitzgerald, and Fats Waller. Staten Island-born folksinger Joan Baez helped to define a generation in the 1960s with her soulful voice and her songs about peace and justice. Queens-born singers Simon and Garfunkel have also devoted much of their careers to singing about life and love in the city. In September of 1981, Simon and Garfunkel held a free concert in Central Park in an effort to raise money to save the Sheep Meadow— a large field of grass in the park that was in danger of being destroyed.

Manhattan has long been one of the country's most popular environments for visual artists. Greenwich Village and Soho have gained reputations for being artist communities, where loft spaces are plentiful and bohemian cafes and coffee shops provide colorful settings for struggling painters and sculptors to meet and talk about their art. Artists like Jackson Pollack, Helen Frankenthaler, and Robert Rauschenberg all worked in New York City in the1950s and 1960s. Later, pop artists such as Andy Warhol used New York as a source of inspiration as well as a home base, further enhancing the city's reputation as an artistic mecca.

ON THE TOUR BUS

Landmarks and Museums
Manhattan

The *Statue of Liberty* is on Liberty Island, in New York Harbor. Though most Americans are as familiar with the Statue of Liberty as they are with the American flag, seeing the statue for real—and being able to explore the inside—is truly a breathtaking experience. Inside the statue, an elevator carries visitors halfway up the structure. Another 168 steps lead all the way to the top of Miss Liberty's crown. The American Museum of Immigration is housed in the statue's star-shaped base.

The *World Trade Towers,* on the corner of Church and Liberty streets, is the world's second tallest building (surpassed only by the Sears Tower in Chicago). It is a vast conglomeration of business offices, stores, and restaurants. An enclosed observation deck in 2 World Trade Center is located on the 107th floor and, on a good day, provides visibility of 75-100 miles.

The *Empire State Building,* Fifth Avenue at 34th Street, is only the third tallest building in the world, but it remains the premier symbol of New York City. Designed by the architectural firm of Shreve, Lamb, and Harmon, the building is a monument to the grandeur and style of Art Deco. Like its cousin, the *Chrysler Building* (42nd Street), its unique style and breathtaking height are thrilling. You can take an elevator almost to the top—1,472 feet in the air—and have terrific views of the island in all four directions.

The *United Nations Headquarters,* First Avenue at 45th Street, is the meeting place for diplomats from all over the world to discuss solutions to global conflicts and problems. One structure, the 39-story *Secretariat Building,* is a simple rectangle of grey steel and glass. Below it sits the nontraditional *General Assembly Building* with its concave roofline and concrete exterior. A semi-circle of flagpoles flying the flags of the U.N. members creates a dramatic entranceway to this building. Next to the General Assembly Building is the *Dag Hammarksjold Library,* a low-lying wide rectangle of large windows and beige concrete. Though most of the offices and rooms are closed to the public, there are multilingual tours.

The *Flatiron Building* was thought of as the world's first true skyscraper, and at the time of its opening in 1901, it was hailed as the tallest building in the world. It is 20 stories high. Located on a sidewalk island created by the intersection of Broadway and Fifth Avenue, the Flatiron is a triangle-shaped structure that follows the lines of the space it occupies. Since its completion, people have argued over what the building looks like. Some think it resembles a large wedge of pie. Others think it looks like an antique iron. Still others think it resembles a ship, sailing up the avenue.

Lincoln Center

Rockefeller Center between Fifth and Sixth avenues at 49th and 50th streets, is a dramatic conglomeration of office buildings and outdoor spaces. *Radio City Music Hall* and the towering *RCA Building* both stand as monuments to the glamour of Art Deco architecture. In front of the RCA Building is a large court that is used as an ice skating rink in the winter and a colorful and beautifully landscaped public space in the spring and summer.

Metropolitan Museum of Art, Fifth Avenue at 82nd Street (East Side of Central Park). An incredible collection of exhibits that span the century as well as the continents, this museum has the largest collection of art and antiquities in the Western Hemisphere. There are 18 departments and over 248 galleries that display over a million prints, paintings, sculptures, costumes, furnishings, ceramics, musical instruments, armor and weapons, and reassembled sections of ancient temples and palaces. In addition, there are three libraries and two auditoriums that offer various programs and movies during the year.

Lincoln Center, 140 West 65th Street and Columbus Avenue, is an impressive collection of six modern concert halls and theaters. It is the home of many of the world's greatest artists and performers. The Metropolitan Opera, The New York Philharmonic, the New York City Opera, and the New York City Ballet all use Lincoln Center as a home base. In addition to their regular performances, the Center frequently hosts visiting performing companies as well as theater productions in its *Vivian Beaumont Theater. Julliard College,* the prestigious college of performing arts, is located in the northern section of Lincoln Center.

American Museum of Natural History, Central Park West at 77th Street, is an incredible collection of over 37 million items. The museum has one of the world's greatest collections of crafts, costumes, masks, artifacts, and animal displays from around the globe.

Museum of Modern Art, 11 West 53rd Street (off Sixth Avenue), has one of the world's most extensive collections of modern art. Beginning with the Impressionists (1880s), this museum houses many of the most influential works created in the past hundred years. Major exhibits of Picasso and Braque are just one of the museum's highlights.

Brooklyn

The *Brooklyn Museum,* 200 Eastern Parkway, is a first-rate museum that rivals the importance of the Metropolitan Museum of Art in Manhattan. The museum has five floors of art and antiquities that span centuries. Major exhibits include arts and crafts of primitive peoples, arts of Asia and Islam, a specialty collection of relics from Dynastic and Coptic Egypt, decorative arts from the seventeenth and eighteenth centuries, and an impressive collection of paintings from many of the major European painters of the nineteenth and early twentieth centuries.

Parks, Zoos, Other Outdoor Places

Manhattan

The Central Park Zoo and Children's Zoo, Fifth Avenue and 65th Street East, is a smaller version of its big cousin the *Bronx Zoo*. Its newly remodeled facility offers well-planned views of seals, monkeys, polar bears, exotic birds, penguins, and many other creatures.

Bronx

The *Bronx Zoo* and *New York Botanical Garden*, Southern Boulevard at 185th Street, is a stunning outdoor collection of over 4,000 animals of 800 species. The Bronx Zoo makes it easy to forget you're in a city. Imaginative settings carved out of stone provide great habitats for gorillas, monkeys, tigers, elephants, and many others. Bison, antelope, ibex, goats, and many other animals from wild Asia and Africa roam large meadows and fields that comprise the 265 acres of the zoo. The *Botanical Garden*, adjacent to the zoo, is another 250 acres of exotic flowers and other vegetation that provides hours of quiet, fragrant walking through magnolia, dogwood, lilac, and rhododendron.

Yankee Stadium, East 161 Street, is a New York institution. Home of the New York Yankees, the "House that Ruth built" is also a monument to many baseball legends, both past and present, including Babe Ruth, Lou Gehrig, Joe DiMaggio, and Mickey Mantle.

Brooklyn

The *Brooklyn Botanical Garden* and *Prospect Park*, 1000 Washington Avenue (Eastern Parkway), is smaller than its Bronx counterpart, but it is still well worth a trip—especially in conjunction with a visit to the *Brooklyn Museum* right next door. The beautifully manicured grounds offer a special garden with fragrances for the blind, another exclusively of roses, one of herbs, and an exotic Japanese garden with wonderful examples of the art of bonsai.

The *New York Aquarium* and *Coney Island*, on the Boardwalk (W. Eighth Street), features sharks, two-ton beluga whales, performing porpoises, and electric eels that light up bulbs. Part of the overall conglomeration of amusements, rides, and other outdoor stands that make up beachfront Coney Island, the aquarium is by far the most interesting and educational element of the area.

Queens

Astoria (Northern Queens) is an interesting neighborhood to experience, though no specific attractions beckon. With the largest central population of Greeks outside Athens, Astoria offers the adventurous diner a wealth of traditional Greek restaurants as well as a number of Greek markets, churches, and cafes.

Shea Stadium, Willets Point (Flushing), is home of the New York Mets. The stadium is easily reached from Manhattan by a 40-minute subway ride. There, one can enjoy a hot dog and some Cracker Jacks, as well as an opportunity to see how seriously New Yorkers take their baseball.

Shea Stadium, home of the New York Mets, is in Flushing, Queens.

Staten Island

The Staten Island Ferry leaves from the Battery (Southern Manhattan). Many Staten Islanders use the ferry for their daily commute in and out of Manhattan. For the visitor, the ferry offers a good opportunity to see both Manhattan and Staten islands from the water—at their most scenic. The ferry trip takes you by the Statue of Liberty and lets you off in one of Staten Island's most scenic neighborhoods.

Five Free Things to Do in New York

A frequent complaint of visitors to New York City is the great expense of touring the island. There are, however, many fun and interesting things to do in New York that are absolutely free. The following is just a brief selection.

• *Free performances of Shakespeare at the Delacorte Theater in Central Park,* which is located around West 81st Street. Joseph Papp oversees two fully staged productions (often using name actors such as Kevin Kline, William Hurt, Glenn Close, and Meryl Streep). The plays run from July through Labor Day.
• *The Schomburg Center,* 515 Lenox Avenue at 135th Street, is one of the world's most important centers for black culture. Contains, among its extensive resources, more than 5,000 hours of historical recordings, films, videotapes, and radio programs.
• *A walk over the Brooklyn Bridge* offers a fantastic view of the Manhattan skyline as well as an up-close look at one of the world's most majestic bridges.
• *A walk through Central Park* in the summer, in particular, offers the casual passerby many diversions, including free concerts and stage performances that are often presented at the park's various outdoor theaters.
• *A Tour of The New York Times,* located at 229 West 43rd Street (Broadway and Eighth Avenue), is a fascinating behind the scenes look at one of the world's busiest and most widely read newspapers. See how the paper is written, edited, laid out, and printed, and hear loads of amazing facts and figures about the paper.

Events

The following is a brief listing of annual events that take place in Manhattan. Many of them are free.

Winter Festival on the Great Lawn in Central Park. Includes snow sculpture contest, winter fashion shows, and skiing demonstrations. Early January.

Chinese New Year in Chinatown. Ten days of fireworks and parades. Mid-January to early February.

St. Patrick's Day Parade down Fifth Avenue. March.

Ringling Brothers and Barnum & Bailey Circus at Madison Square Garden. Late March.

Ninth Avenue International Festival with exotic foods from countries and cultures all over the world. Mid-May.

Puerto Rican Day Parade on Fifth Avenue above 59th Street.

Festival of St. Anthony with games and street fairs throughout Little Italy. Early June.

The Kool Jazz Festival at various locations around the city. Late June–early July.

Independence Day Festival in lower Manhattan. July.

Free outdoor music and entertainment in Lincoln Center. August.

New York Book Fair on Fifth Avenue. Mid-September.

The New York City Marathon, the biggest. Last Sunday in October.

Macy's Thanksgiving Day parade. November.

The lighting of the Christmas tree in Rockefeller Center. December.

1524	New York Bay discovered by Giovanni da Verrazano.
1609	Henry Hudson first explores the river that is later named for him.
1626	Dutch leader Peter Minuit buys the island from the Manhattan Indians.
1639	Jonas Bronck settles the area that becomes the Bronx.
1643	First permanent settlement in Queens established at Flushing.
1654	First permanent Jewish settlement in North America established in New Amsterdam.
1664	The Duke of York sends a British fleet into the harbor to take possession of New Amsterdam.
1725	*Gazette* begins publishing.
1735	Trial of John Peter Zenger establishes principle of free press.
1754	The population of the city is more than 16,000 people.
1775	The American Revolution begins, placing all the colonies at war with Britain.
1781	Colonies win the war against Britain.
1789-1790	Manhattan serves as first capital of federal government.
1789	The first president of the United States is elected, sworn in at Federal Hall in Manhattan.
1790	The first U.S. Census records more than 30,000 people in New York City.
1812	The United States and Britain fight over Canadian boundaries.
1825	Erie Canal opens.
1830	The great wave of immigration from Europe floods the city until 1860.
1834	The city of Brooklyn is incorporated.
1840	New York is leading port in the nation.
1858	Work on Central Park begins.
1861	The Civil War begins; New York fights for the Union.
1874	City's boundaries are expanded.
1883	The Brooklyn Bridge opens to traffic.
1885	The Statue of Liberty is dedicated.
1898	New charter adopted, five boroughs become Greater New York.
1904	First part of subway system opens.

1914	World War I breaks out in Europe.	1950	The Korean War begins.
1918	The war is over; prohibition and women's suffrage sweep the country.	1952	The United Nations opens its headquarters in New York City.
1920	The Harlem Renaissance begins.	1953	The Korean War comes to an end.
1929	A stock market crash in October sends the country reeling into the Great Depression.	1965	John V. Lindsay is elected mayor; New York struggles through the political unrest of the 1960's, with protests against Vietnam and protests for civil and women's rights.
1930	The Empire State building is completed.		
1933	Fiorello LaGuardia is elected mayor.		
1939	World's Fair opens at Flushing Meadow.	1974	World Trade Center twin towers are completed.
1941	The United States enters World War II after Japanese bomb Pearl Harbor.	1977	Edward I. Koch elected mayor of New York City.
1945	World War II is over and peace and prosperity return to America.	1989	New York elects David N. Dinkins, the city's first black mayor.

For Further Reading

Appleberg, Marilyn J. *I Love New York Guide.* Simon & Schuster, 1985.
Bailey Livesey, Herbert. *The American Express Pocket Guide to New York.* Prentice-Hall, 1985.
Hamilton, Marian. *The Best Things in New York Are Free.* Harvard Common Press, 1987.
Seret, Roberta. *Welcome to New York.* Doubleday, 1985.
The WPA Guide to New York City. Pantheon Books, 1982.

Where To Get More Information

New York State Department of Commerce, Tourism Office: (212) 827-6100
"I Love New York" Office of Tourism and Travel Information: 1-800-225-5697
New York City Department of Cultural Affairs Information: (212) 974-1150
New York City Visitor's Bureau: (212) 397-8200
New York City Office of Tourism: (212) 827-6255

INDEX

Photo credits

All photos by Bruce Glassman except for:
Pages 3 (middle), 28-29, 36, 38, 41: Private Collection; p.10, 20, 58:
courtesy of New York Convention and Visitor's Bureau; p.31: New
York Public Library, I,N. Phelps Stokes Collection; p.33: New York
Historical Society; p.34: Museum of the City of New York; p.42:
Brooklyn Historical Society; p.47: Joan Vitale Strong, Photographer to
the Mayor; pps. 53, 54, 55, 56: UPI/Bettmann Newsphotos.